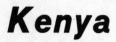

Kenya

← A FIRST BOOK →

Kenya

by F Blanche Foster

illustrated with photographs

Franklin Watts, Inc.
575 Lexington Avenue
New York, N.Y. 10022

Special thanks are due to the Permanent Mission of Kenya to the United Nations

Photographs courtesy of:
F Blanche Foster: page 47 bottom
Kenya Information Services: cover, frontispiece, pages 4 top, 8, 14, 17, 22, 28, 32, 37, 49, 50, 53, 55, 56, 58, 59, 66, 68, 72, 73
Anthony D. Marshall: pages 9, 11, 16, 19, 20, 21, 45, 51, 65, 71
New York Public Library Picture Collection: page 25
Three Lions: pages 4 bottom, 6, 13 (by Alice Schalek), 30, 35 (by Alice Schalek), 36 (by Alice Schalek), 39, 41, 43, 63
United Nations: pages 47 top, 60, 69
United Press International: page 61

The selection on pages 23-24 is reprinted with permission of Doubleday & Company, Inc., and is taken from *Old Africa Rediscovered,* by Basil Davidson, published by Doubleday: Toronto, 1959.

Map by George Buctel

Contents

To members of The International Afro-American Museum
Kwa hivyo tutafanikiwa tukivuta pamoja.
"Thus let it be that success
will come as we pull together."
— Jomo Kenyatta

Kenya

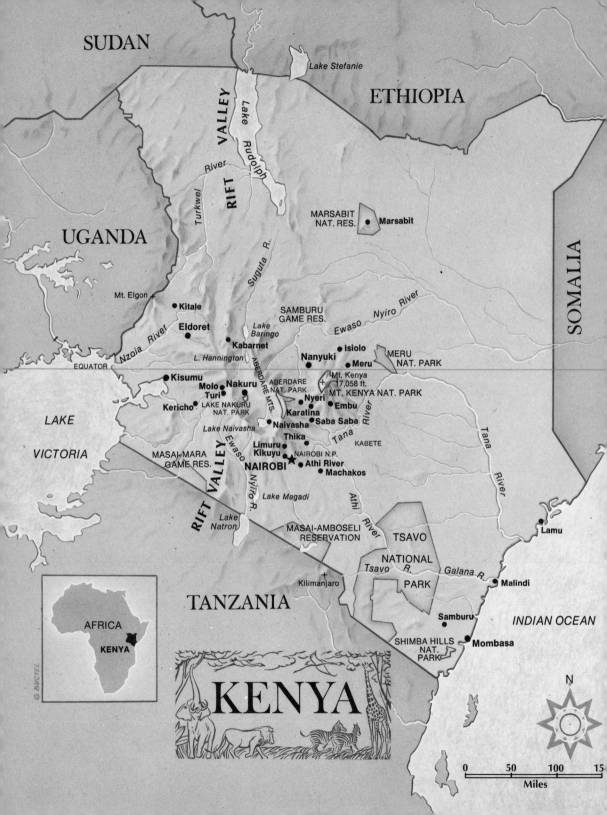

SUDAN

Lake Stefanie

ETHIOPIA

RIFT VALLEY

Lake Rudolph

Turkwel River

Suguta R.

MARSABIT
NAT. RES.
● Marsabit

UGANDA

SOMALIA

Mt. Elgon

Nzoia River

● Kitale

Eldoret ●

● Kabarnet

Lake
Baringo

L. Hannington

SAMBURU
GAME RES.

Ewaso   Nyiro River

EQUATOR

● Kisumu

Molo ● ● Nakuru
Turi ●

Kericho ●

LAKE NAKURU
NAT. PARK

ABERDARE
NAT. PARK

ABERDARE MTS.

Nanyuki ● ● Isiolo
        ● Meru

Mt. Kenya
17,058 ft.
MT. KENYA NAT. PARK

MERU
NAT. PARK

● Nyeri
● Karatina
Saba Saba ●
Naivasha ● ● Embu

Lake Naivasha

Thika ●

Tana River

KABETE

Limuru ●
Kikuyu ●
NAIROBI ★ NAIROBI N.P.
        ● Athi River
        ● Machakos

Tana River

MASAI-MARA
GAME RES.

RIFT VALLEY

Ewaso

Nyiro R.

Lake Magadi

Athi River

Lake
Natron

MASAI-AMBOSELI
RESERVATION

TSAVO

NATIONAL

Tsavo R.

Galana R.

● Lamu

● Malindi

PARK

LAKE

VICTORIA

TANZANIA

Kilimanjaro

KENYA

AFRICA

KENYA

G. BUCTEL

● Samburu

INDIAN OCEAN

SHIMBA HILLS
NAT.
PARK

● Mombasa

N

0   50   100   15
      Miles

Uhuru

In the African language Swahili, *uhuru* is the word for freedom. Throughout the African country of Kenya, *uhuru* implies a rich, historic past and a thriving present for every citizen. *Uhuru* means that all of Kenya's people shall be forever free. *Uhuru* also implies protection and love for Kenya's animals, birds, and natural beauty.

The struggle for freedom in Kenya is symbolized in the national flag. This striking banner, containing a shield with crossed spears in the center of its three stripes of black, red, and green joined by two white bands, is a graphic symbol of uhuru: black for Africans; red for the blood that was shed during the struggle for independence; and green for the fertility of the land. The white bands are called bands of unity. They unite the people, their struggle for independence, and the land. The crossed spears are re-

3

The Kenya national flag is placed on Mt. Kenya as the clock strikes midnight and Independence Day — December 12, 1963 — begins.

During the Mau Mau rebellion all Kenyans suspected of belonging to the Mau Mau were rounded up and placed in barbed wire compounds.

minders that freedom is worth fighting for. Freedom is so important to Kenyans that the national constitution has a bill of rights to ensure freedom from slavery and forced labor, freedom of conscience, and freedom of movement.

Uhuru has not always been a word black Kenyans could utter openly. Before the secret organization Mau Mau terrorized the land and made it obvious that Kenya must be returned to black Africa, uhuru was the word whispered to give meaning and strength to black Kenyans in their quest for freedom from white British rulers.

When the British settled in Kenya in the early 1900's, they moved into the fertile lands, driving most of the tribes to a poor and far less cultivable area infested with tsetse flies. Although there were many fights between the British and the various tribes, it was not until some effects of Mau Mau terror were felt that the British decided to act upon demands of black Africans. Between 1952, when the Mau Mau rebellion brought about a declaration by the British of a state of emergency, and 1963, when Kenya gained independence, many changes were made. Uhuru became a word of fear to the British. By 1963, "Uhuru Kenya!" was being shouted across the land.

The Mau Mau secret organization, which proclaimed freedom as a goal for Kenya, was a movement of resistance to white supremacy. The organization consisted mainly of

5

Kikuyu tribesmen who had suffered great losses of land and human dignity at the hands of the British. The leader and champion of the movement for the struggle for independence, Jomo Kenyatta, became the first Prime Minister of Kenya on June 1, 1963, following the May election victory of his party, KANU (Kenya African National Union). Through these elections the overwhelming majority of Kenyans strengthened Kenya's bid for uhuru. The British submitted to the will of the majority, and Kenya became an independent nation on December 12, 1963. Twelve months later, when Kenya became a republic, Kenyatta became the first President.

President Kenyatta's road to freedom for black Kenyans was a difficult one, beset with both pitfalls and rewards. A brilliant scholar and handsome statesman, Jomo Kenyatta perhaps felt the first exciting thrust of uhuru over seventy years ago as he learned from his grandfather, a witch doctor, and other elders about the glorious past and the strength of the Kikuyu.

Kenyans demonstrate to demand freedom for Jomo Kenyatta, who was convicted as the Mau Mau leader. Upon Kenya's independence, Kenyatta became the country's first Prime Minister.

Independence celebrations at Uhuru Stadium in Nairobi, on December 12, 1963, see Jomo Kenyatta sworn in as Prime Minister of Kenya.

Kamau wa Ngengi was President Kenyatta's name at birth. It meant Kamau, son of Ngengi. After Kamau studied in a mission station near Nairobi, he received a Christian name, Johnstone, which he later dropped in favor of the Swahili *Jomo,* which means "burning spear." Even freedom to change his name was important to him.

Many years later, when Kenyatta became President of Kenya, one of his first acts was to change some names in his newly independent country. Kenya became the name of the land that was formerly known as British East Africa. Many streets and boulevards throughout the cities and towns received names which reflect a struggle for freedom. Uhuru Street is one of the most important thoroughfares in several of Kenya's cities. Kenyatta Boulevard, Haile

Kenyatta Boulevard in Nairobi.

Selassie Drive, Nkrumah Boulevard, Nyerere Street, and other streets have been named in honor of African leaders. These are the men who led the fight of Africa's suppressed peoples for freedom. In Kenya today, freedom is a reality. Uhuru exists.

The Land of Kenya

Nature endowed Kenya with unusual physical beauty. However, the breathtaking features of the land are so rugged that they have been tamed only through great human wisdom and strength. The country covers an area of 224,960 square miles, including about 5,300 square miles of water. Although located on the equator, much of Kenya does not have the hot unpleasant climate usually associated with equatorial areas.

Kenya is a country blessed with a variety of environments. In the mountains and highlands the climate is cool and the farmland is fertile. Running from Kenya's northern boundaries with Ethiopia and the Sudan to its southern boundary with Tanzania is the Great Rift Valley where the climate is tropical. The valley starts at the mouth of the Zambezi River, which flows into the Indian Ocean, then continues northward through Kenya, crosses Ethiopia,

10

*The Great Rift Valley extends through Kenya from Lake Rudolf
in the north to the Tanzania border in the south.*

going to the coast to form the floors of the Red Sea, the Gulf of Aqaba, and the Dead Sea. It ends in Syria. The valley is like a deep gorge or trench in the earth resulting from a series of breaks, or north-south fractures, in the African continent. It was formed during the uplift of the continent long before man was believed to have arrived there. The earth movements that caused the formation are linked with volcanic activity. In Kenya, the valley is thirty to forty miles wide. Small extinct volcanoes dot its floor. There are several lakes in the valley, including Lake Rudolf, one of the largest in Africa.

In addition to the highlands and the Great Rift Valley, Kenya has areas of thornbushes, dry savanna (largely tree-less plains), and semidesert. On the east coast, where miles of palm trees give way to the Indian Ocean, it is hot and humid.

Much of Kenya's turbulent history is closely related to its topography and location. On the southern border lies Tanzania; on the west are Lake Victoria and Uganda; in the northwest corner is the Sudan; on the north is Ethiopia; and on the eastern border are Somalia and the Indian Ocean. The topography and location gave rise to the formation of different tribes, dictated the mode of living, and today play an important role in Kenya's economic and political life.

The harbor at Kilindini, on the east coast.

Luo tribesmen fish on Lake Victoria in the west.

The highlands of Kenya form an important area since at least 85 percent of the country's entire population live there. Prior to independence in 1963, the area was populated mainly by Europeans who drove the native inhabitants away so that they might occupy the highlands, with their cool climate and fertile soils.

The highlands — more than five thousand feet above sea level — are formed by lofty mountains like the beautiful snowcapped Mt. Kenya, Africa's second highest mountain, which reaches an elevation of 17,040 feet. Located east of the Rift Valley, this fertile highland area is called the heart of Kikuyuland. Mt. Elgon, an extinct volcano west of the Rift Valley on the Uganda border, reaches a height of 14,178 feet. In the Masai lands of southern Kenya, one can see Africa's highest mountains, the Kilimanjaros, in neighboring Tanzania. In the southwest, near the Aberdare Mountains where Sattima Peak reaches 13,104 feet, lush greenery and waterfalls give the land an air of peace and serenity.

The savanna regions are important because the Europeans forced many of the native inhabitants to live there in the grasslands, or so-called bush. These regions are *low* grassland and thorn scrub and *high* grassland with scattered trees. Kenyans value this area, although the venomous reptiles, preying animals, and parasitic insects that infest

This European house in the Rift Valley was owned by ex-Governor Sir Philip Mitchell.

Mt. Kenya, the nation's highest mountain (17,040 feet), is the second highest mountain in Africa.

the bush make the land especially dangerous for human beings. Perhaps the survival of Kenyans in this dangerous land adds meaning to their belief in animism. Animism is a kind of religion which basically believes in soul — soul of a mountain, lake, tree, or of any living thing.

Only 3 percent of the population live in the semidesert area of the north. Lake Rudolf, the largest lake in Kenya, is located in the Rift Valley. Although it is one of the

Fishing in Lake Rudolf.

most beautiful lakes of Africa, few people have seen Lake Rudolf because the land around it is so hot and full of hazards.

Tucked in scenic and paradise-like areas are other lakes, waterfalls, rivers, springs, and caves. Lake Hannington is a small lake in the Rift Valley. On its shores many geysers may be seen. Lake Nakuru is often covered with so many flamingos that its waters appear to be pink. Lake Naivasha, near Nairobi, also is rich in birdlife. Lake Victoria is the third largest lake in the world. The Kenyan port of Kisumu is located on Lake Victoria. Caves like the Suswa Caves are relics of the age of volcanoes. Bats, baboons, and leopards have lived in these caves for thousands of years.

The main rivers of Kenya are the Athi, Tana, Suguta, Nzoia, Ewaso Nyiro, and Galana. Some of these are permanent and others are seasonal rivers, which are often dry until the rainy period arrives.

When the Europeans settled in Kenya, the fertility of the highlands, the scenic landscape, and the abundant wildlife enchanted them. Long before their arrival the Masai tribe had mastered the art of herding sheep and cattle, but this was a difficult task for the first Europeans in Kenya. Even mere survival in the land was not easy for them.

Agriculture and cattle herding had always been a way

Elephants on the Ewaso Nyiro River.

of life for some of the native tribes. The Europeans attached an economic value to what the land could produce. Although Kenya's mineral resources were minimal, proper use of natural vegetation yielded great profits. Such crops as cassava (a tropical root vegetable), yams, bananas, coconuts, and maize (corn) were abundant. Plantations were established for producing coffee, tea, and sisal, the cactus-like tree from which fiber is extracted for making rope, carpets, twine, and sacks.

Kenyans have a love for the land. The circular native

Sisal, used in making such things as rope, carpets, and sacks, is grown on large plantations.

homes blend with nature in patterns of color. The pastoral gentleness and love of the highlands and savannas are expressed in well-cultivated hillsides. The castlelike anthills, the "upside-down" boabab trees, the cattle, the wild beasts, and the Kenyans themselves unite under the immense sky, valleys, and mountains of their land.

Zamani (*Long Ago*)

Some historians and anthropologists believe that the first man (Homo sapiens) lived hundreds of thousands of years ago in the country known today as Tanzania. Many of these people migrated northward into what is now Kenya. Fossils and remnants of early man discovered at Olduvai Gorge have led to the belief that all mankind began there. Evidence of Stone Age man — his bones, the bones of animals he ate, pots and bowls, and his weapons and tools — has been found in the Rift Valley near Nakuru, and can now be seen at the museums in the capital city of Nairobi.

Several hundred years ago voyagers from different countries sailing the Indian Ocean came to the east coast of Kenya. They came from Egypt, Arabia, Persia (known today as Iran), China, and India in search of timber, ivory, and spices. Later voyagers from Europe came searching for trade too. The traders brought cloth and beads which were sometimes exchanged for ivory and slaves.

Dr. Lewis Leakey, who discovered remnants of early man in the Great Rift Valley of Kenya, as well as in other parts of East Africa, examines a twenty-million-year-old animal jawbone.

President Kenyatta looks at thirteenth-century Arab monuments at a historical site.

As early as A.D. 975 Persians had settled in Kenya. Many Arabs who had sailed to Kenya in dhows also settled there. Dhows, which were known in ancient times, are still used in the port of Mombasa. They are wooden boats with a deck covered in the front, a single mast, and a large triangular sail. It was not unusual for these Arabs to marry African women. Their children were called Swahili, a word derived from the Arabic "as-sawahil," meaning "the coasts." They spoke Swahili, a mixture of Bantu and Arabic languages.

A gross misconception that Africans were uncivilized heathens incapable of producing a great civilization has been allowed to penetrate the pages of Western history and to distort the truth about black Africans. The truth is that the Europeans who came to Africa five hundred years ago were much impressed by the towns, wealth, and the people they saw. Historian Basil Davidson set the record straight in his book *Old Africa Rediscovered*:

> They went ashore to cities as fine as all but a few they could have known in Europe. They watched flourishing maritime trade in gold and iron and ivory and tortoiseshell, beads and copper and cotton cloth, slaves and porcelain; and saw that they had stumbled on a world of commerce even larger, and perhaps wealthier, than anything that Europe knew.
>
> To these European sailors of the last years of the fifteenth century the coast of eastern Africa could have seemed no less civilised than their own coast of Portu-

gal. In the matter of wealth and knowledge of a wider world it must have seemed a great deal more civilised. They were repeatedly surprised by the ease and substance of the ports and towns they saw and sheltered in and plundered. They found themselves repeatedly disregarded as strange and uncouth. "When we had been two or three days at this place," says the laconic log-book of da Gama's flagship, the *São Gabriel*, of an encounter at a port that was probably Quelimane (above the Zambesi River), "two *senhores* of the country came to see us. They were very haughty; and valued nothing which we gave them."

Around 1500 the Portuguese, in search of a seaway to India, came to Kenya's shoreline on the Indian Ocean. Two of the well-known voyagers were Vasco da Gama and Francisco de Almeida. The Portuguese, determined to establish trade routes on the Indian Ocean, built forts along the ocean shores. They wanted to control the slave trade and other trade for huge profits. They tried to destroy the trade of the Arabs who had come long before them. Bitter fighting occurred between them. In 1590 the Portuguese built Fort Jesus, a stronghold which protected them in the harbor of Mombasa.

The people of Kenya did not like the Portuguese, because they were intolerant of the inhabitants and their religion. The Portuguese did not make friends easily among the Muslims and Hindus, and it was not very long before the Omani Arabs overtook the Portuguese and drove them from Mombasa and other ports. Their final defeat came in 1699.

The use of human beings as slaves — people in servitude against their will — had existed in East Africa for many years before the arrival of the Europeans. However, the slave owners before the Europeans generally did not treat their slaves as chattel. In fact, slavery sometimes offered a

Arabs and Africans enslaved and traded Africans.

new opportunity to people who were left destitute and without families following a war or famine or other catastrophe; it was not unusual for Arabs and African slave owners to marry their slaves or to make them a part of their families.

Many Arabs did make huge profits from selling slaves. The slaves were taken in dhows to Arabia, India, and other lands. They suffered inside the dhows because they were packed like fish in a basket. Africans seeking to sell ivory were often captured and sold along with their ivory.

Arab slave traders came to fear the Masai warriors, who would attack the slavers whenever possible and free their captives. But for the most part the native tribes, grouped as they were by region, beliefs, and kinship, were disunited and poorly organized militarily against the guns and weapons of the slave traders.

Many horrible and macabre tales have been told about the slave trade. There are stories of young boys and girls forced into slavery, of women ripped apart, and of children thrown into great bonfires.

The British and Portuguese organized their slave trading differently from the way the Africans had. The African was more protective of his slaves. He did not disrupt homes and separate families merely for his own profit. To the British and Portuguese only the "bodies" were important.

26

The hideous and profitable practice of slave trading was officially ended by British law in 1807. Many traders continued the business, however, until the British outlawed the practice of slavery in 1833. Although slavery and the slave trade were discontinued in the British Empire, both existed in British-dominated East Africa until 1897.

Before the Swahili and Arab coastal traders came into the region near the Rift Valley and before the "sharing up" of East Africa, there were well-developed tribal ways of life suitable to Kenya. Each tribe had its own form of government, dress, weapons, food, language, religion, and customs. The family unit was strong, and the children were made to feel secure and loved. The system of the extended family both protected members of the clan and tribe and created bonds of unity in a common struggle for survival. Moreover, no child was ever without a family. Polygamy, or the taking of several wives by one man, was and still is a pattern of the extended family. This helps ensure the family lineage, the care and protection of the young, and the dividing of the work.

Since the people of Kenya migrated from neighboring areas like Uganda, Somali, and Egypt, there were naturally many differences of tribal custom among them. The features of the land they inhabited also dictated such things as dress and food. Some pastoral tribes moved from one

These village youngsters are given a feeling of security through the warm companionship of other children and adults.

area to another, constantly seeking fertile soil, while others were agricultural and tried to maintain permanent settlements.

There were dynasties and kingdoms among the tribes. The kingdom of Wanga played a great political role in western Kenya from about 1598 to 1895. Some of the rulers were Nabongo (Spiritual Leader) Wamukoya Netya (1760–1787), Nabongo Wamukoya (1814–1841), and Nabongo Shiundu (1841–1882). One dynasty was called the Abashitsetse Dynasty. The last Nabongo of Wanga, Mumia, lived until 1949.

When the Europeans came to Kenya, they brought with them their pictures of a white Savior. But many of the tribesmen preferred their own religions. The Kikuyu tribes, for example, worshiped the god Ngai, associating him with the beautiful snowcapped Mt. Kenya. Some of the tribes worshiped their dead ancestors. Africans had their own ideas of god and worshiped according to their mode of life. Many of the tribes disliked the teachings of the missionaries and many missionaries were killed. The Africans could see how the Catholics and Protestants fought each other and how Catholics and Protestants together fought the Hindus and Muslims.

Missionaries began exploring the interior of Kenya around 1849. The German missionary Johann Ludwig Krapf told of seeing Mt. Kenya and the snow on top of the mountain. Since this mountain is so near the equator, many people found his story somewhat incredible. Soon many European nations became interested in East Africa, and countless Dutch, German, and British explorers and missionaries came. Between 1880 and 1885, East Africa was partitioned, or divided, among the Europeans. Kenya was called British East Africa and was declared a British protectorate in 1895.

Many tribes in Kenya did not like the British. First the Masai fought them, but in 1895 they became friends. Other

Before independence British soldiers with submachine guns were a common sight on city streets.

tribes also fought the British but were subsequently conquered. The British established military and civil stations in such territories as Baringo, Naivasha, Kisumu, and Fort Smith (Nairobi). In order to withstand external threat, the British had to maintain good relations with the black Kenyans. African chiefs thus retained control of their districts but the British firmly controlled the chiefs.

The British formed companies, established factories, built a railroad, introduced their modern communications systems, and began the exploitation of the land and people of Kenya. Indian laborers, traders, and clerks, who make up a large portion of the Asian population, also stayed.

Since economic gains depended to a large extent on cheap African labor, it was necessary for the British and Indian people to learn the language of Kenya. When they did, they quickly put into practice Swahili phrases which were demeaning to the human quality of the Kenyans. Such words and commands as *bwana* (master), *Nijibu* (Answer me), *Nipishe* (Let me pass), *Mtumishi mwema we* (You are a good servant), *Mtumishi mbaya we* (You are a bad servant), and *Usinijibu* (Don't answer me back) became widely used by the European to keep the Kenyan in a subservient role. Very little attempt was made to educate the Kenyan. It was the old idea of "If you don't let them learn they will not earn!"

31

While rehearsing for a pre-independence television program teaching Swahili, the instructor points to the word bwana *(master).*

The People of Kenya

During the period of British colonialism, the people of Kenya lived under a caste system with almost no social contact between racial groups. The system was similar to that which existed in the United States during slavery and to that which exists today under South Africa's policy of apartheid, or total separation of races. Asians in Kenya were given positions in trading and clerical fields while Africans were relegated to the lowliest jobs.

The African fought in both world wars, but it was only during World War II that he made new relationships with people outside Africa. Upon his return home, he yearned for the freedom he had fought to establish for others and for better opportunities in his country's business and social life. The caste system was an affront to his abilities and intelligence. Although the British built statues honoring the

33

bravery of the African, the words engraved on them offered little consolation for his being denied full participation as a citizen in his own land.

Statues in honor of black Africans who died fighting for freedom in World Wars I and II may be found in Kenya's cities. Inscribed in Arabic, Swahili, and English, such words as the following are usually found engraved on the tablet at the base:

This is to the memory of the Native African troops who fought . . . to the carriers who were the feet and hands of the army and to all other men, who served and died for the King and country in the great war, 1914–1918. If you fight for your country, even if you die, your sons will remember your name.

| 1914 | 1939 |
| 1918 | 1945 |

Since independence and the rise in the effectiveness of the black African's protest, the composition of the population has been changing. Today's population is estimated at about 9,670,000. Approximately 9,400,000 are African, 200,000 Asian, 40,000 Arab, and 30,000 European. Although non-Africans are eligible for citizenship, many are returning to their former homelands of Britain, India, and

This monument to black soldiers who fought in World War I was brought to Kenya from England.

Pakistan rather than becoming citizens under black rule. Racism is so deeply ingrained in some of these people that they actually prefer to seek new homes in strange lands than to remain in a Kenya that has guaranteed equal rights to all.

In Kenya, as in most of Africa, tribal differences have been played up by the colonialists. By keeping the people divided the colonial powers found it easier to conquer and

An Indian shopkeeper walks through Old Mombasa, which has a large Indian population.

rule. Claiming that the Luo, for example, are endowed with certain mental capabilities and that the Masai are warlike yet clever tends to disunite the people. When the colonizers called upon chieftains of various tribes to carry out their mandates, they would point out to each chief that his tribe was "different."

Tribes are similar to various national groups, such as

A Masai homestead is decorated with headdresses for a feast.

Irish, Swedes, Alsatian French, German Bavarians, and so forth. Kenya's tribal divisions continue to play a dominant role in the political, social, and economic development of the country.

Many people know about the Masai tribesmen. Much has been written about their customs, art, herdsmanship, and their resistance to change. Actually, the Masai is one of the smaller tribes of Kenya. There are approximately fifty-five tribes in the country, the largest of which is the Kikuyu. Some other tribes are Luo, Luhya, Kamba, Meru, Kalenjin, Kisii, Embu, Turkana, Kamasia, and Taita.

Today, most tribes remain in areas which they inhabited long ago. Many Kikuyu and Luo, however, live in large cities and towns with other Kenyans and with immigrants from other African countries. The Masai live mainly on the Amboseli Masai Reservation in the south, although some members of this nomadic group may be seen in areas very near Nairobi.

The Asians originally came to Kenya from India and Pakistan. They live mainly in the large cities of Nairobi and Mombasa. Today, relations between the Asians and Africans are strained because many Asians are not willing to accept Kenyan citizenship. Under colonial rule the African was kept out of Asian trades, religions, and politics. The

This mosque in Nairobi is a reminder of the Arab involvement in Kenya's history.

Asians kept a closed society which since independence must be open to all citizens.

The Arabs live in the cities, towns, and villages of the Indian Ocean coast. Kenyans maintain better relationships with the Arabs than with the Asian population because many Arabs have married Kenyans and have accepted their culture.

Europeans live in the highlands and areas where commerce, agriculture, and ranching flourish. Since independence many Europeans have returned to their former homelands or are searching for a new homeland in other countries. Many of their former holdings in Kenya have been bought by the Kenyan government for African settlement and development.

Skin colors are as varied in Kenya as are her tribes, languages, and climates. The average Kenyan looks like any other person of mixed African heritage, or much like the Afro-American. He may be any one of nature's various shades of brown and black, ranging from fair to brown to

Nairobi's streets show signs of many cultures — Arab-owned shops, African people and patterns, and the English and Western styles.

dark, soft black. Facial features range from the so-called Caucasoid to Negroid or Asian.

Kenyans vary in size too. Like all people, they are short, medium, or tall. Different tribes are generally identifiable by their headdress, ear marks, facial marks, or dress. That, of course, refers only to those who have not decided to become completely Westernized.

Kenyans dress in several styles. Western attire, however, is the most fashionable and is worn even in rural areas. Styles for many Kenyans still include the *shuka* (a togalike garment), *kikois* (a wrap), shawl-covered faces, bare breasts, and the Nigerian-like *gele-buba-iro* (head tie, blouse, and wrapper). Almost everywhere one sees brightly clad Africans holding their bodies erect and carrying baskets or wares on their heads.

Cities and Towns of Kenya

Kenyans, like people all over the world, live in cities and towns. Some, however, still live in the bush, which is similar to the backwoods, swamplands, and mountainous areas of the Americas.

*More and more modern buildings are sprouting up in Nairobi.
Beyond the bus terminal one can see Government Road.*

The Masai tribesmen gave to Kenya's largest city the
name Nairobi, which means "the place of the cool water."
Nairobi is the capital of Kenya and enjoys a prominent role
in the political, commercial, and industrial activities of
Africa. Situated about 5,500 feet above sea level, Nairobi is
where cattle, agriculture, and culture flourish.

43

It has been said that Nairobi came into existence almost by accident. When the Uganda Railway was being built, a group of workers and traders had set up tents and shanties in what is now Nairobi. The original plan was to bypass the site by eight miles, but the route was changed and the railroad came through the present-day city. The trains brought people who built the city with its beautiful buildings, highways, and gardens.

Along Government Road and Harambee Avenue are the elegant government buildings, which, for the most part, have been constructed since independence. Embassies, consuls, and high commissions are located near and on Kenyatta Avenue.

Nairobi is a center for both business and industry. Some of the chief industries are engineering, tire and battery making, flour milling, baking, furniture making, tobacco processing, and beer, soap, and glass making. In nearby towns there are factories for making shoes and cement.

On the doorstep of the city is a game park where lions roam, leopards wander, and hippopotamuses lounge lazily in the pool. Zebras, impalas, and gazelles move leisurely in the park of Nairobi.

Mombasa, Kenya's oldest city, is one of the largest ports on the east coast of Africa. Originally built on a small coral island, Mombasa has spread to the mainland. Today it

Giraffes in Nairobi's national park.

combines the exotic past of Arabian Nights, Hawaiian serenity, Oriental aromas and colors, busy waterways, and African realism into one of the most exciting cities in the world.

President Kenyatta made this Indian Ocean port a vital part of Kenya. He initiated the practice of holding state meetings in Mombasa and built a home there. One of the main streets near the Indian Ocean is Mama Ngina Drive named in honor of Kenyatta's wife.

Huge elephant tusks stand at the entrance to the city's commercial area and seem to invite you to enter. Not far from the tusks is Uhuru Fountain, one of the main symbols of African independence. It was built in 1963, the year of Kenya's independence. Constructed in the shape of the African continent, it is decorated with bright colors and the Mombasa coat of arms.

Small boats and dhows are still seen sailing the waters around Mombasa. As the largest port of Kenya, Mombasa exports to other countries such items as coffee, tea, the insecticide pyrethrum, and sisal. Some of her imports include oil, bicycles, shoes, cars, and metals.

Mombasa has many thriving businesses and factories. Africans there make beautiful carvings and other works of art, jewelry, and clothing. The city's factories produce cans, soap, paraffin, paint, sugar, glass, paper bags, and cement.

Surrounding Mombasa are miles of palms, pale sandy beaches, and stately mansions fronting the blue-green shores of the Indian Ocean. Little native villages dot the gorgeous landscape. Their colorful African houses harmonize with the pure shades of the soil, shrubbery, palm and coconut trees.

*A street scene in Mombasa, Kenya's oldest city and one of the
largest ports on the east coast of Africa.*

*Huge elephant tusks stand at the en-
trance to Mombasa's commercial area.*

Nakuru is one of the rich farming towns in the Rift Valley. Situated between the extinct Volcano Menengai and Lake Nakuru, Nakuru is the home of the Kenya Farmers' Association. Most of its industries are associated with agriculture. Much wheat, sisal, and maize are grown there. Each year a large two-day agricultural show is held in Nakuru.

Kisumu, on famous Lake Victoria, is the important western port of Kenya. Notable are its fishing centers, soap factories, sugar refineries, and engineering industries. Annually, large crowds gather in Kisumu for a two-day cattle and trade show.

Other towns in Kenya have musical-sounding names such as Eldoret, Nanyuki, Meru, Kitale, Thika, Nyeri, and Naivasha. The clever Kenyans in Sabasaba took the name of their village from a conspicuous 7-Up sign. "Sabasaba" is Swahili for "7-Up."

Both near to and far from the cities and towns, there are thousands of Kenyans inhabiting the bush. Although people there are somewhat removed from the swift pace of modern Kenya, their pleasant faces and erect bodies reflect the same sense of national pride that one sees in urban areas. It is in the bush that much of the glorious past of Africa is still cherished and immortalized through local customs.

The bush people learn easily and early the ways of sur-

At Kisii, located in the west, farmers benefit by joining together to form a cooperative association.

In a western village everyone joins in a traditional tribal dance.

vival. A sense of responsibility is taught to the very young, along with training in education, religion, and etiquette.

The little houses of the bush sharply contrast with the newly designed apartment buildings and homes that stand in the cities and towns. But the modern bicycles on the footpaths suggest the easy adaptability of these Kenyans to the changing world.

In the rural areas and farming sections like Karatina and

Circular houses can be seen in Kenya's villages.

Large crowds gather at marketplaces such as this one in Karatina.

Kirinyaga, men and women take pride in their products. Since many of the men work in factories in the cities and towns, the women and children are often left to care for the farms. On Saturdays they can be seen carrying their produce to the markets, where Kenyans gather to buy, sell, and visit.

Serikali (*The Government*)

When Kenya became independent in 1963, the British government relinquished its power. The old form of government based on British lines was modified to embody Kenyan principles of democracy.

Kenya is divided into districts or counties. Districts combine to form provinces, of which there are seven. The National Assembly represents the people. In 1966 the Senate and House of Representatives merged into what is now the National Assembly. The President and members of the National Assembly, elected by the people, make up the ruling body of Kenya, its Parliament.

The Kenyan Constitution has as its cardinal rule that "there shall be no discrimination whatsoever based on race, tribe, color, religion or place of origin." The Constitution was designed to meet the needs of the people and the governing body.

52

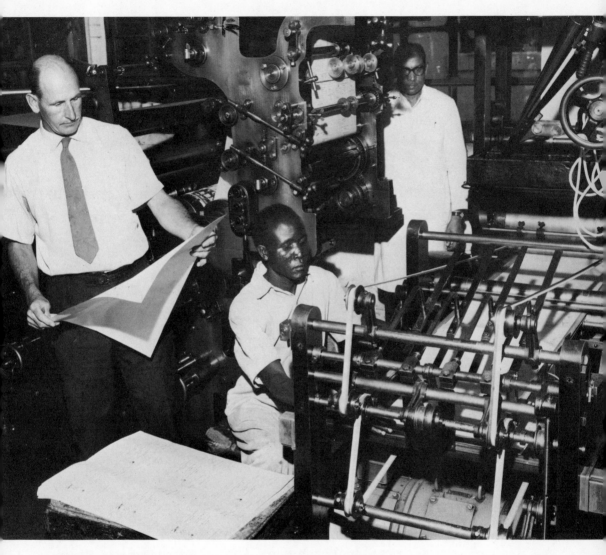

Printing ballots for the country's first election in 1963.

Before Jomo Kenyatta became President, he had been elected Prime Minister on the KANU (Kenyan African National Union) party ticket. The Constitution was amended to make Kenya a republic and Mzee Kenyatta the first President of the land. The Swahili word "mzee," which literally means "old man," has been made an honorary title given to Jomo Kenyatta.

According to the Constitution, the President is elected by the people. Each political party taking part in the general elections nominates one candidate for President. Each nomination must be supported by one thousand registered voters. When more than one candidate is nominated a poll is taken in each constituency for the election of the President and the candidate who receives a majority wins. Requirements for the office of President are citizenship, a minimum age of thirty-five, and qualification as a voter.

The Vice-President is appointed by the President, and must himself be a constituency member of the National Assembly. During the absence of the President, the Vice-President has all the status, responsibilities, and powers of the President.

The spokesman for the National Assembly is the Speaker, who is elected by Parliament. The ceremonial mace, a beautiful work of African art wrought in gold and ivory, is the symbol of the constitutional authority of the National As-

The government owns and operates Kenyatta National Hospital in Nairobi.

sembly. It is carried by the Speaker and rests on the table of the chamber while he is in the chair.

Parliament is charged with enacting legislation, or law-making. Ministers and government departments execute, or carry out, the laws. The judges and magistrates decide if a law is broken. The Supreme Court is the highest court of the land. Ministers of the government of Kenya have

55

responsible positions and must report to the National Assembly.

The government has the difficult task of building and staffing schools and hospitals, and is in charge of housing, transportation, and roads. Maintaining a stable economy is both very important and difficult. To do this, Kenya relies

A government-sponsored housing project.

upon her sales, taxes, and grants, as well as loans from other countries. Most Kenyans over the age of eighteen pay a graduated personal tax. Married women are exempt from the tax.

In spite of all the work the government has to accomplish, the welfare and spirit of the people are of special concern. Parliament is responsible for passing legislation that will give Kenyans added pride in themselves and in their new nation.

Pulling Together (Harambee)

Kenyans have a word which keeps before them their method of meeting the challenge of change. *Harambee*, or pulling together, resounds throughout the Republic to give strength, vitality, and purpose to Kenyans: They are pulling together toward their goals.

Education is given a high priority in Kenya. There are public schools in all cities and towns. Children living in rural areas also have schools. Kenya now has many elementary schools and several high schools which are nonsectarian. In addition, many schools organized by religious missionaries remain open. College and university attendance is high. Some of the schools of higher learning include

With the cry "Harambee!" a self-help group works to build a road.

A teacher helps his students at an elementary school.

Asian and African students at University College in Nairobi.

Nairobi's University College, Kenya Polytechnic Institute, Kenyatta College of Teacher Training, College of Social Sciences at Kikuyu, and College of Veterinary Science, Kabete. One of the goals of Kenya's education is "learning to live together."

Health services are fast improving. Hospitals and clinics can be found throughout the country. A mobile clinic services patients in rural areas by flying into sections of the bush.

Athletes are highly regarded in Kenya. The country is

proud of such world-famous track stars as 1968 Olympic gold medal winners Naftali Temu, Kipchoge Keino, and Amos Biwott. In all, Kenya's 1968 winter Olympics track and field team won eight Olympic medals. Kenya's boxers are admired also. Some of the better boxers are Philip Waruinge, John Nderu, Peter Manene, Lawrence Kariuki, Stephen Thega, and Stephen Baraza. Football and tennis draw many fans throughout the country.

The mass media in Kenya are facing the challenge of change. The content of the press, movies, radio, and television never before represented the culture of the black people, but efforts are now being made to eliminate any-

Olympic gold medal winner Kip-choge Keino (on right).

thing which does not have a wholesome effect on African culture. A consciousness of the psychological effects that words may have has resulted in the reconstruction of words that were tainted with overtones of racial prejudice. For example, the word "redmail" is now used instead of "blackmail."

The press is attempting to identify itself with the country and the people. Kenya has four daily newspapers, three in English and one in Swahili. Books and magazines are published both in English and in Swahili. There is a great need, however, for more publishing. The love of reading is evident everywhere — Kenyans can be seen lying on the ground or standing on corners reading books, newspapers, and magazines.

English is still the official language, but most people speak Swahili and a tribal language. It is hoped that in the future Swahili will become the intellectual, social, and cultural voice of freedom. The literary spirit of Kenya is growing through such English-language writers as Khadambi Asalache, Lennard Okola, Okello Oculi, and Duncan Gichangi. The literary journal *Ghala* (Swahili for granary, reservoir, or depository) focuses on the cultural and intellectual pursuits of the country.

Kenyans are not overlooking the educational and recreational aspects of movies, radio, and television, but they are

A radio broadcast at the new Broadcasting House studios in Nairobi.

changing their content to reflect the life, culture, and people of black Kenya. Plans are under way to feature black Kenyans in movies that will replace the cowboy, gangster, and sex films, which are considered to be bad models for the people. Both radio and television are emphasizing informational and educational programs.

In radio there is a national service which begins at six o'clock in the morning and is programmed mainly in Swahili. The general service is in English. The radio fare consists of such programs as "A Day in Parliament," "News,"

"Music of Africa," "Light Music," "People and Places," "Students' Magazine," "Open End/Citizens Want to Know," "Africa Today and Tomorrow," "Jazz Special," and "Theatre."

Television programs begin at five-thirty in the afternoon. A typical day's program looks like this:

Today's TV

5.30 PROGRAMME PARADE
5.35 CARTOON TIME
5.45 STAR SOCCER
6.45 KORTI YA KIBERENGE
　　　(Kiberenge's Court)
7.15 HABARI NA MAELEZO YAKE
　　　(News and Commentary)
7.35 THE LUCY SHOW
8.00 TIME FOR MUSIC
9.30 HABARI NA MAELEZO YAKE
　　　(News and Commentary)
9.50 CINEMA

The national spirit since independence has revived and revitalized the classical art, dance, and music of the Republic. Schools are urged to teach African songs and dances.

64

Kenyan arts and crafts on sale at a factory outside Nairobi.

Dance drama is popular, and opera with African music and lyrics is being developed into a fine art.

The functional art of old Kenya is compatible with the modern art, as each expresses an interpretation of African heritage. The old art uses traditional designs as decoration on household items, such as leather garments, wooden ves-

sels, and gourds. Its strong influence can be seen in the abstract art of the Western world. Wood carvings and beadwork of Kenya are sold in many parts of the world. Some of Kenya's modern artists include Elimo Njau, Samuel Wanjau, Eli Kyeyune, Okot p'Biket, Ntiro, and Mwaniki.

Since independence there has also been great progress made in the business world. Racial tensions and pressures in past employment patterns gave black Kenyans limited managerial and executive opportunities. Although Kenya is mainly an agricultural and farming country, its people have already shown their abilities to establish and maintain other business ventures. Some examples of successful African industrial and commercial enterprises include: Thika General Workshop, which manufactures water tanks, cans, gutters, and general tinsmith articles; Mbooni Timber Saw Mills in Machakos; Nduati Saw Mills near Limuru and Wood Working and Joinery at Turi near Molo; African Diesel Injection Service in Nairobi, which does a variety of service jobs for the motor vehicle industry; Maendeleo ya Wanawake Organization in Nairobi, which sells handmade curios to tourists; and the Typewriter Sales Service in Nairobi, the first African company in Kenya to obtain an international typewriter agency in East Africa. Plans and investigations are under way for the completion of other Kenyan businesses.

67

Tin articles are manufactured at Thika General Workshop.

The Kenyan government is investigating its mineral resources in hopes of strengthening the economy.

Tourism is also a business in Kenya. Just as Switzerland "sells" her lofty mountains, and the West Indies their beaches and pleasant climate, so does Kenya "sell" her landscaping, mountains, waters, and animals. People from all parts of the world help Kenya's tourist business by visiting game parks, lakes, and cities as they study and watch the wonders of nature there. They also come to hunt big game, to study birds and insects, to fish, and even just to relax.

The many national parks and game reserves of Kenya are located in a variety of climates and scenery. Names of some of the parks and reserves are Tsavo, Amboseli, Meru, Nairobi, Masai-Mara, Samburu-Uaso Nyiro, Marsabit, Shimba, and Lake Nakuru. National parks are also found in the mountain ranges of Mt. Elgon, Mt. Kenya, and the Aberdares. In Aberdares National Park there is a hotel built in the trees in the heart of the wild-game land where visitors watch in amazement as herds of elephants, buffalo, waterbuck, and rhinoceros walk together and frolic at the water hole.

As Kenyans pull together, too, finding confidence and assurance in the value of their goals of national progress, they still find time for relaxation in their parks, stadiums, places of amusement, and markets. Throughout Kenya, Saturday is a day of joviality when throngs of people, cars, buses, and wagons jam the marketplaces. Sunday generally

*The long-legged secretary bird found in Kenya is a bird of prey
that lives mostly on reptiles.*

Tourists at the Tsavo National Park watch from their lodge as an elephant drinks from a nearby pool.

finds Kenyans attending churches of their choice. The legal
holidays, similar to those of many countries, include Good
Friday, Easter, Labor Day (May 1) in honor of Kenya's
workers, Independence Day (December 12), and Christ-
mas. Kenyans also observe Madaraka Day (June 1) to celebrate the attainment of internal self-government before

*Students at the Kikuyu Girls Secondary School celebrate Christ-
mas with a play.*

independence, August Bank Holiday (first Monday in August) when banks close to take stock, Kenyatta Day (October 20) in remembrance of Kenyatta's arrest in 1952 and the declaration of a state of emergency, and Boxing Day (December 26), a traditional British holiday.

Today, thanks to Jomo Kenyatta, "Great Father of the Kenyan Republic," all citizens of Kenya have the legacy of strength imbued in the words "uhuru" and "harambee." A likeness of Kenyatta's face is seen in every public place, on the currency, literature, and in homes. The example of his achievements — independence and progress — should unite Kenya's leaders and people and guide them to greater glories.

Bibliography

Barton, Frank. *The Press in Africa*. Nairobi: East African Publishing House, 1967.

Davidson, Basil. *Old Africa Rediscovered*. Toronto: Doubleday, 1959.

The East African Institute of Social and Cultural Affairs. *East Africa's Cultural Heritage*. (Contemporary African Monographs Series, No. 4.) Nairobi: East African Publishing House, 1966.

————. *Racial and Communal Tensions in East Africa*. (Contemporary African Monographs Series, No. 3.) Nairobi: East African Publishing House, 1966.

————. *Research Priorities for East Africa*. (Contemporary African Monographs Series, No. 5.) Nairobi: East African Publishing House, 1966.

75

Moore, Clark D. and Dunbar, Ann, editors. *Africa Yesterday and Today*. New York: Bantam, 1968.

Slade, Humphrey. *The Parliament of Kenya*. Nairobi: East African Publishing House, 1967.

Were, Gideon S. *A History of the Abaluyia of Western Kenya*. Nairobi: East African Publishing House, 1967.

Pronunciation Guide

NOTE: "g" has a hard sound, as in "good"
"ow" rhymes with "now"
"th" is soft, as in "thanks"

Abashitsetse — ah *ba* shee seh seh
Amboseli — ahm boe *seh* lee
Athi — *ah* thee
Baraza — ba *ra* za
Baringo — ba *ring* go
Biwott — bee *watt*
Bwana — *bwa* na
Eldoret — *el* dor et
Elimo Njau — el *lee* moe en-*jow*
Embu — *em* boo
Ewaso — ee *wa* so

77

Galana — ga *la* na

Ghala — *ga* la

Gichangi — gee *chan* gee

Habari na Maelezo Yake — ha *ba* ree na ma *yell* eh zo *ya* kay

Haile Selassie — *hi* lee seh *la* see

Harambee — ha rahm *bay*

Jomo — *joe* moe

Kabete — ka *beh* tay

Kalenjin — ka *len* jin

Kamasia — ka ma *see* ya

Kamau wa Ngengi — Ka *mow* wa en-*gen* gee

Kamba — *kahm* ba

Karatina — ka ra *tee* na

Kariuki — ka ree *oo* kee

Kenya — *ken* ya

Kenyatta — kin *ya* ta

Khadambi Asalache — ka *dahm* bee ah sa *la* cheh

Kikois — kee *ko* ee

Kikuyu — kee *koo* yoo

Kipchoge Keino — keep *choe* gay *kay* no

Kirinyaga — kir een *ya* ga

Kisii — kee *see* ee

Kisumu — kee *soo* moo

Kitale — kee *ta* leh

Korti ya Kiberenge — *core* tee ya kee bare *en* gay

Kyeyune — kye eye *oon* eh

Limuru — lee *moo* roo

Luhya — loo *hie* a

Luo — luh *woe*

Machakos — ma *cha* kos

Madaraka — ma da *ra* ka

Maendeleo ya Wanawake — ma en del *ay* oh ya wa na *wa* kay

Manene — ma *nehn* ay

Mara — *ma* ra

Marsabit — *mar* sa bit

Masai — ma *sye*

Mau Mau — *mow mow*

Mbaya — um *bye* ya

Mbooni — um *boo* nee

Menengai — *meh* nehn guy

Meru — *may* roo

Molo — *moe* loe

Mombasa — mom *ba* sa

Mtumishi mwema we — um too *mee* shee um *weh* ma way

Mumia — *moo* mee ya

Mwaniki — um wa *nee* kee

Mzee — um *zee*

Nabongo — na *bone* go

Naftali Temu — nahf *ta* lee *tay* moo
Nairobi — nye *roe* bee
Naivasha — nye *va* sha
Nakuru — na *koo roo*
Nanyuki — na *new* kee
Nderu — en *dehr* roo
Nduati — en doo *a* tee
Ngai — en *guy*
Ngina — en *gee* na
Nijibu — nee *jee* boo
Nipishe — nee *pee* sheh
Nkrumah — en *crew* ma
Ntiro — en *tee* roe
Nyerere — *neh* reh reh ee
Nyeri — nye *eh* ree
Nyiro — nye *ear* o
Nzoia — en *zoy* a
Okello Oculi — o kel *loe* o *koo* lee
Okola — a *koe* la
Okot p'Biket — o *kot* bi *kat*
Sabasaba — sa ba *sa* ba
Samburu-Uaso Nyiro — sam *boo* roo oo *ah* so nye *ear* o
Serikali — ser ee *ka* lee
Shimba — *shim* ba
Shiundu — shee *oon* doo

Shuka — *shoo* ka
Sondu — *son* doo
Suguta — soo *goo* ta
Swahili — swa *hee* lee
Taita — *tay* ta
Tana — *ta* na
Thega — *they* ga
Thika — *thee* ka
Tsavo — *tsa* voe
Turi — *too* ree
Turkana — *tur* ka nuh
Uganda — you *gan* da
Uhuru — oo *who* roo
Usinijibu — oo *see* nee jee boo
Wamukoya — wa moo *koe* ya
Wanga — *wan* ga
Wanjau — *wan* jow
Waruinge — wa roo *een* gay

Index

83

84

DATE DUE

MAY	9 1978		
OCO3 '89			
JN 31	JAN 1 3 '94		
	JAN 1 1 '95		
OCT 3 8 2006	OCT 1 9 2006		
	Withdrawn From Ohio Northern University Library		
GAYLORD			PRINTED IN U.S.A.